ABOUT THE AUTHOR

David Mason has worked as an immunopathologist, a sales training manager and has owned a restaurant. He began writing in 1993; his first book was produced in 1996. He works in schools teaching children how to be terribly dramatic and write stories and poems. He has six wonderful children and a lovely wife. They live in Norfolk in a happy, noisy house

D1437974

"Metaphor Man" © David J. Mason 2008
Publishing address: North Street Publishing
1 Millfield Road, North Walsham, Norfolk NR28 0EB
Telephone: 01692 406877   www.InspireToWrite.co.uk   Email:
DavidMasonPoet@AOL.com

By the same author:

"Inside Out"	Poetry 1996
"Speaking Out"	Audio collection 1997
"Get a Life"	Poetry 1997; illustrations by Nick Walmsley
"Seven Summers"	Poetry 1998
"Leo's Magic Shoes"	Children's novel 1999; Illustrations by Kirsty Munro. Reprinted in 2000 as "Pedro's Magic Shoes" with illustrations by Nick Walmsley
"The Great Sweetshop Robbery"	Children's poetry 2001
"Handy Andy has the Candy"	Children's poetry 2001
"Go Teddy Go"	Children's CD poetry-songs 2002
"The Elf who sang the King to sleep"	Children's fables and fairy tales 2002
"Living in another world"	Children's poetry 2003
"Teacher's Cauldron"	Children's poetry 2004
"When..."	Children's poetry 2005
"Two into one"	Children's poetry 2006 Reprinted 2008
"The White Book"	Children's poetry 2006 Reprinted 2008
"Learning to Fly"	Children's novel 2007
"Metaphor Man"	Children's poetry 2008

Printed by JEM Digital Print Services Ltd
Staplehurst Road, Sittingbourne, Kent ME10 2NH
www.jem.co.uk

Table of Contents

4

When

When the sight of a small child
Ceases to stir some love in me
When the brilliant sunrise
No longer excites my soul
When the distant horizon
Is a solid black line
When the whispering trees
No longer talk to me
When the big bright flowers
Are just another set of colours
When the mountain and the valleys
Merge to one great plain
When some sad words or tune
Don't make me feel pain
When the sea spray smell
Means no more than lifeless sand
When my children's touch
Stops at my hand

When the food in my mouth tastes
As if I've had enough already
When my eyes are forever
Bigger than my belly
And the only greed I know
Is to have more money
When faceless fear has
Finally overcome me
When I am deaf

To the cry of humanity
When I am blinded
And close minded

When I can never make the effort
Because I am too tired
Or dwell too long in comfort
And never step outside
When I cannot
Taste success
When I cannot
Smell danger

When I can no longer
Think for myself
But am deafened by
Ideas of other men
(And the secondhand words I speak
Are those dull, uttered on some main street)
When science and statistics
Cause me to surrender
And I believe that the world
Begins and ends here
Then it is time
To put me
In a dark box
And label it
"Here he lies,
Dead to the world".

Diary of a conker

<u>Friday 20th September</u>

Bad night, last night
Couldn't get to sleep
Tossing and a-turning
Under spiky green sheet.
The wind whistles round me
The branches reel and sway
Squeak and creak and sudden snap
A slender thread gives way.

<u>Saturday 21st September</u>

Today I lie concussed
And bruised about the head
My front and back and sides they ache
My battered arms and legs.
My shell it has burst open
The air is bitter cold
This is all quite natural
Or so I have been told.

<u>Sunday 22nd September</u>

Now I fear I'm lost
In the dark I cannot see
Stuffed deep in a pocket
They ran away with me.
Two boys they said
   – We'll string him up
   He looks a real winner.

He's big and brown, his shiny skin
I'll bet he packs a punch, yeah!

Monday 23rd September
They drill straight through my brain
And push my insides out
Then they thread the shoelace
And pull the noose up tight
– Put him in the oven first
It'll make him better
Yeah will bake him hard as bricks
Skin as tough as leather.

Tuesday 24th September
I'm all dressed up for action
I'm ready for the fight
Mean machine of muscle
Heart as dark as night.
They put me head to head
With a big guy just like me
I swung down on him from above
Smash him to smithereens

Thursday 3rd October
I'm a hundred-and-sixty-four-er
And life is tough and hard
I crush them in the playground
Fight duals in the park.
There is no end to this I say
It's kill or die yourself

But how I wish I could escape
And live a peaceful life.

Saturday 19th October
Today must be my last
I've lost a limb or three
I'm cracked, I'm split, I'm finished
Death would bring relief

Sunday 20th October
Still they want to swing me
I'm hanging by a thread
I'm dazed and bruised and badly cut
About my conker head.
...I'm losing it, I'm punch drunk
It's time to end this story
I'd like you to remember me
Thousand-and-sixty-four-er
Who retired at the pinnacle
Of a conquering career
Ascended to the heavens
To make chestnut trees up there.

For sale

Humanoid occupied planet
Per-Cambrian registered
Six hundred and fifty million years old
Several careful occupiers
Except greedy humanoids
MOT'd till 2020
Pollution needs attention
As does American nation
Hence reduced price
Good little orbiter

Would part exchange for new home

Must have clean water and air
No previous history of humanoids there
Also planning permission for new humanoid race
Unlikely to make the same earthly mistakes.

Serious business
No time wasters please. Contact:
The Creator
Heavens Above
www.thinkaboutthefuture.com

Global Warning!

When the grey cloud of smog thickens so
That we can hardly breathe
And the green house gases choke so
That the earth begins to heat
So that there's no escape from the warmth of the sun
And the melt of the glaciers has now begun
So that the sea level rises by and by
And great lakes lie where the land was once dry.

When the low-lying villages are first to go down
Then next it's the fields and the woodlands that drown
And finally Holland is one inland sea
(In the UK we've moved to the mountains and hills)
Then, and only then

I shall swim all the way to London
With a waterproof petition
And ask the Admiral of HMS Houses of Parliament
If he wouldn't mind admitting there's a problem.

Bed

My daughter is really attached to her bed,
I'm never, ever leaving it – she said.
To bed on New Year's Day each year
For full twelve months – she stays there.
It's homely, warmly, cosy, comfy
But sleepwalking on the streets is bumpy.

She says that it's discrimination
Time for you to wake up nation
Understand the plight of those
Whose bodies shrouded in bed clothes
Will never, ever leave their nest
And live their life like all the rest
Take the taxi, aeroplane
Sleep over at a friend's again.

My daughter is really attached to her bed,
A trial separation, we said.
The tears, the emotion, agony on leaving
From the depths of her only home she is heaving
Herself says it all up here in her head
Try sticking to something else
Instead...

My daughter attached to our settee
Soft and slinky on castor wheels
And when she's rolling steady and slow
We shout at her – Couch Po-ta-to!

Missing pants

You can't tell – at a glance
That I'm not wearing – underpants.
It's not by chance
I have no pants.

No, it is upstairs perchance
Baby's sleeping with my pants.
And it's sleep the baby wants
Not me looking for my pants.

Some say that it's a song and dance
And we don't need to have our pants.
But I'm not one to take a stance
And prance around without my pants.

For one can tell with one swift glance
When one's not wearing underpants.

Metaphor Man

Come on down here, Metaphor Man
My composition it's an also-ran
You can do the things that simile can't
Inspirational metaphor, Metaphor Man.
Save me, save me
And my story
Metaphor, metaphor
I believe, see!
Come on down from your metaphor cloud
With your abstract suit and your metaphor sound.
Save me, save me
I have to change it
Metaphor, metaphor
And rearrange it.
I worked it all out, say I have the plan
All I need is a metaphor from Metaphor Man.

Explaining the weather

This evening the heavens
Were pitch black
The shining stars of Hollywood are
Never coming back.

Christmas, there won't be
Any snow at all
For feather flakes are scared of heights and they
Don't want to fall.

It was the end of
The cold snap
For the greedy crocodiles stopped biting
The ice cap.

This longest summer
So baking hot
For all the angels chefs and commis were cooking
Such a lot.

There was not a breath
Of wind outside
For the wind had stopped breathing
And died.

There was not a
Cloud in the sky
For God he clipped their wings and wingless
Clouds won't fly.

There was not a
Drop of rain
For the holes in the sky have been
Blocked again.

We haven't seen the
Sun for days
For the sun is too hot and must
Hide in the shade.

But there was never
A moon so bright
As the one we wrapped in silver foil
And hung out in the night.

Queen

Oh queen, great queen,
Where have you been?
I've been to my people
To see the unseen.

Oh queen, our queen,
What did you see?
I saw hopelessness
I saw poverty
I saw thirst and hunger
Disease and death.
Faceless bodies
Shadows of themselves.

Oh queen, great queen,
What did you hear?
Moaning and groaning
And splashing of tear
A painful silence
A cry of despair.
An awful screaming
A living nightmare.

Oh queen, so queen
What was the smell?
The stench of fear
The taint of hell
A taste of want

That none can tell.
Sinking under
Gravest spell.

Queen, oh queen
What shall be done?
Pray for them
Each and everyone...
... ...
... Sell my silver
Sell my gold
Take my crown
And royal robe.

Oh queen, no queen
What shall remain?
Leave me nothing
But save my life
Let me know
This people's plight.
For I must touch
The unseen life.
And share with them
Their darkest night.

The case of Galaxy Smooth-Silk

Taken the short distance from
Her prison cell
She arrived at court looking
Surprisingly well
Sporting the latest design
In wrapper
Faced up to the jury
Looking dapper.

This chocolate treat
Radiant fashion
Defended her case
With stubborn passion.
The judge would not listen
He slammed down the hammer
And turned to the jury
His eyes full of anger.

The accused before you
Is plainly guilty
She's much too smooth too
Soft and silky
She's chocolate temptress
Through and through
Why, she's a danger
To all of you.

Just one look at that
Perfect outer
And all you can do is

Dream about her.
Do you Galaxy have
Something to say
Before this court doth
Lock you away.

I'm sorry, your Honour it must be my dress
That makes me appear a chocolate temptress.
Your Honour not guilty
Is what I will say
Why not close your eyes or
Just look away?
I think you know the
Answer to this
There's no person living who
Can resist

That velvet outer
And textured inner
That creamy chocolate
Running river.
Galaxy Smooth you
Are sentenced today
To die in the
Most appropriate way.

You shall not hang
But this fate instead
The judge and jury
Will bite off your head
And slowly, but surely
Suck you to death.

21

Pen-friend

Wanted: Pen friend to share in exciting times

My interests are:
Simply staring or
Sleeping in and watching
TV and paint dry.
Couch potatoes and comas.
Drinking dull dishwater.
Eating ready salted crisps.
Sometimes getting up
And going to the toilet.
Making nothing out of something.
Toe twitching, finger stretching.
Clock watching.
Nail filing, hair growing.
Plain speaking, stamp licking.
Gentle breathing, heart beating,
Distant gazing,
Eye glazing,
Patiently waiting
For your reply.

Premiership poetry

Premiership poetry pays well,
Sponsorship writes my name on pens.
If I'm injured falling from the stage
And damage my poetic head
They'll bring on a substitute poet
To perform poetry in my stead.
I want to play poetry for England
In front of sixty thousand fans
At the Stretford Road End.
I want to compete in Europe
And play some Portuguese poetry.
I'd like to train at La Manga in Spain.
When I retire in my early thirties
With a gravelly voice and worn out verses
I shall teach some poetry
At the National poetry academy
Where poetic youngsters
Can learn about the game,
The heartache, the money,
The fortune, the fame.

The Good Samaritan – a youth from North Walsham

Two a.m. and the polystyrene outer
Take away home of chips and burger
Is tossed aside by the shady owner
Of a speeding, clapped-out souped-up Rover.
What careth I? He says to his sordid self
And leaves the victim to die a lonely death.
Two a.m. and a little bit,
Outer tries to crawl for it.
The bin, the bin – gotta reach the bin
Can't make it – someone gotta put me in.
Two a.m. and a little bit more,
Outer in the darknes – hopeless, forlorn.

Seven a.m. sees the rising sun
At eight a.m. footsteps have begun
To sound upon the footpath loud
Where lies polystyrene adjacent in the road.
Gaily skips by a man from Council offices,
Head full of figures and next year's budgets,
Sees polystyrene but passes by,
You must another's help to try.
For I in sooth am far too busy than
To bother with ridding streets of litter.

Second there passes a gentleman
Elderly with a middle-aged suit on.
He takes one look at polystyrene outer
And side-steps quickly over to the other

24

Side of the road where safe he is
From passing youth, these dangerous kids
Who if he were to stop for outer
Would jump upon and duff him over.
That is why we employ a street cleaner,
He says to himself, feeling much better.
By and by there stumbles an awkward youth
With multiple piercings and a cigarette in his mouth.
He squints against the brilliant sun
And wishes to go back to bed again.
Through haze that polystyrene shape,
Alas poor outer, I must put him away,
For the bin is less than two metres distant
And the rubbish it needeth a home to live in.
And the youth he cradled the polystyrene outer
And put him in the bin for collection later.
So I ask you my friends, which was the good neighbour?

Living for the presents

Do not look to tomorrow
For the present is your concern
And the past – don't dwell too fast
For living in the present is what you must learn.
That's me I live for the present
I took the prophets at their word
Any other way to live
Is frankly quite absurd.
Birthday's need a countdown
Six months before the day
I'm planning on the presents
The ones that you can buy.
Christmas starts September
(Well it's the same in) all the shops
We're living for the presents
I'm sure it pleases God.
All the things we had before
They're presents of the past
And here within my cosy home
They weren't built to last.
I don't think of the future
Beyond the present list
For life without the presents
Does surely not exist.

But I hear that there's some people
No food or running water
No presents left to hope for
Their hope lies in the future.

Strange when Jesus left us
He said, "You'll know my presents",
But maybe he meant rich people
And not the lowly peasants.

I'm one of the lucky ones
The present is for me
But take away my present
I've nothing else to be.

Tough guy

Who's in and who's out?
What's this shouting all about?
The loudest noise
The biggest mouth
I'm in
And you're out!

The bestest dress-test
The coolest style
I'm the winner
By a mile.

The hardest kick
The toughest head
You're the worst-est
I'm the best.

Tallest story
Longest lie
You so low down
Me so high.

Mostest muscles
Tough and mean
Skinny yours
All stringy bean.

You're a mouse
And me a lion
You of tissue
Me of iron.

I'm the streetwise
You're the scared
I broke the rules
And never cared.

Who's in and who's out?
That's what life is all about.
The shaking fist
The pointed finger
The sweaty hand
That holds the trigger
The boots that squash
The words that hurt
The heart of nails
Poison, dirt.

Who's in and who's out?
The silence screamed, I've lost the bout
What I am is paper thin
Shred me and begin again.

I'm out and you're in
Those who shout can never win.

Recipe for an English Winter

Take a magnificent Mediterranean sun
Dilute ninety-nine parts to one.
One that burned so fierce a yellow
Now a pale English shadow.
Tame those beams in misty glass
Lock them in a cupboard dark.
Storm clouds pass of black and bold
Eastern winds of frozen cold.
Frost and hail, ice and snow
Snuff the warmth of golden glow.
And now that jar so long forgotten
Smells of winter's something rotten.

The cloud

Bold dawn breaks
Clear and blue
A memory
A ghost to you.

Angel threads sown
Cotton sheet white
I creep across the skyline
Unfolding into sight.

Merging blanket pale grey
Black smudge between the lines
Bubbled tar on stormy tides
Hoarse the wild wind whines.

A candle's flame
A jigsaw sky
Clouds retreating
By and by.

I am a cloud,
I am crystal, I am gas
Invisible I colour,
Precipitate and pass.

When I grow up

My parents are always saying to me
That being an adult
Means responsibility.
That long word is
Worrying about others
And shouting orders.
Then your head aches
And you can't sleep
And there isn't even
A moment's peace.

You have to have responsibility
At home and at work
All day during daylight
And all night when it's dark.
Responsibility is something
You take seriously.
You are not born with it
They make you learn it.
It is a disease of the mind
The adult kind of mind.
It can drive you mad!
My Mum and Dad
Say I'm lucky not to
Have caught responsibility
But it will eventually
Catch up with me.

I'm asking me
What'll I do
When I grow
I don't really know –
I'll make it my mission
To take a responsible decision.

Yes, when I grow up
I don't want to be an adult.

At the little beach

When silvery beams
Dance on jet black –
Time to take a peek
To pull the curtain back.
Then to reveal
The fishes moon-bathing
Mermaid audience
Sipping, champagning.
Watching as the
Theatre unfolds
Stories of sea knights
At night time are told.
This afternoon's wrecks
Of half-made castles
Are whole once more
Therein live damsels
In deep distress
Rescued by knights
Their moonlit swords
Are flashing white lights.
Slaying sea monsters,
Who live in the deep
So all the goodies
Might dwell here in peace.
Fearless they're fighting
The dragon's hot fire
Saving these soft sands
From dark and despair.

These guardians of truth
The boldest and brave
Bring light to this beach
On the crest of a wave.
Their sea horse chargers
Fast galloping foam
Shadows on these waters
Till the blessed daylight comes.
And the knights and their castles
At daybreak are jaded
The waves washed the beach
And the mystery faded.

Please Miss

Wearing his smile so serene
The little lad
At the back of the classroom
For one fleeting moment
Catches my eye,
A worried expression paints over his smile –
And a tear drop floats
And clouds his sky.
He turns to me
As if in a dream
Slowly but surely
He paddles upstream.

Weaving his way 'twixt children and desks
Bravely determined
To take all the risks
His face made graver by the minute
Our messenger boy
Has hidden within it
Something so terrible, something so shocking
As to shorten the breath
And to stop the heart ticking.
As if in a dream
Slowly but surely
He creeps towards me.
What is the secret he harbours within?
That taunts and haunts
And unsettles him
Such a small boy, such a big load
His body is aching

His soft back is bowed
Pray, deliver the hurt from your soul.

Tell me, teacher, you know you want to
Is it another boy who hit you?
Maybe a tragedy happened at home
The dog is not well or the budgie has flown
A crime you committed they'll never forgive
Locked up in prison as long as you live.

Perhaps a bomb dropped
'pon your home
And all your favourite
Toys are gone
No money, not a crumb of bread
A fear of never being fed
The water's off, the standpipe's on
Fear is here, all hope is gone
Nuclear winter, global warming
Came today without a warning

Limp he wilts in a pool of tears
I've helped him understand his fears.
Hapless, yes I know him well
Gently does it, he will tell.
Come dear child stand at ease.
With trembling hand and shaking knees,
"Miss, can I go to the toilet please?"

You are what you eat

Chorus:
Quality fruit and vegetables
Quality fruit and vegetables
Quality fruit and vegetables
They're the ones for me.
Sha-la-la-la-la-la dee dee
You are what you ea-eat
Sha-la-la-la-la-la dee dee
Yes you are what you eat, eat!

I go to the chocolate
Get sick in me tummy
A sicky feeling
This confectio-nary
I think I'm a going
To throw it up see
No more chocky please
No confectio-nary!

Chorus
I go for the burger
It stick me all up
I swallow the burger
It sticks in me gut
Dis constipation
Is gluing me
No more burgers please
It is constipating me!

Chorus

I go for the cola
It's acid bath
I rinse round with cola
Dissolving me mouth
Dis cola fizzy
It's rottin' me teeth
No more cola please
Rottin' all me teeth!

Chorus

I go for the colours
They look so pretty
But those coloured sweeties
They turn me dizzy
Makin' me fly
Like a bird in the tree
No more colours please
Hyper and dizzy!

Chorus

Lily

Floats the scent of lily flower
Heaven sent celestial power
Beaming bright and warming rays
Yellow hazy lazy days.
Chemical caress and kiss
Leaves soak up the summer bliss.
Magical this transformation
Nectar, honey sweet sensation.
Inhaling deeper I can find
The clear blue corners of my mind.

Listen up

The air guitar, a funny thing
Air without and e'er within
Straining hard to strum a sound
The music made is so profound.

I learnt to play my air guitar
No-one thought I'd go too far
But look at me – a huge success
Our air band – it is the best.

We've air bass and we've air drum
We've air lead and per-cussion
Air keyboards and amplifiers
Air support band standing by us.

And now we've gone and named the band
"We are The Air!" we tell our fans.

"Turn it up man, we can't hear!"
Air step up to higher gear
Rock star look on rock star face
Fingers riff and rhythmic bass.

We play mean and we play harder
Our hands are flapping even faster.
"Man that's good, hey we dig you!"
"Man The Air can really groove!"

And that's the secret of success
That's what makes The Air the best
At every gig you're headache-less
Hear every word you ever sez.

Stinking Sid

Stinking Sid, the garlic kid
Tongue of herb and spice
Yellow teeth and burning breath
Skin of curried rice.

Miss she said, "Well come on Sid
Have mercy on our noses,
We'll plant you in the flower bed,"
Now Sweet Sid smells of roses.

I'll give you a clue

There's addition and there's take away
Lots of hidden signs
Thousands of those numbers
On millions of those lines.
There are teachers and assistants
To help you on your way
Books of endless questions
Until your dying day.
It's serious
There are no laughs
Have you guessed?
It's mental
Maths.

Got to get speaking proper

Couldn't get to sleep
Got up
Got dressed
Got my breakfast
Got my things ready
Got on the bus
Got off again.
Got to rush
Get there just in time
Got to go to assembly
Got to sit patiently.
Got to lessons
Teacher's got to teach
Hasn't got anything better to do
Always gets the better of us, though.
Got a mean temper, got a big brain
Says we've got to listen to him.
Got to open our exercise books
He's got one of his funny looks.
"Right, you class, just sit
And write me a story
Without the word 'got' in it."

Grandma

A kiss on paper thin skin
Be careful not to crush the ribs
A fragile heart beats
On thin pin limbs.
Grandma is shaking with excitement
A little unsteady but smiling
Warm to the touch
Grandma's not ready for dying.
I sit upon her knee
I listen to a story
Grandma tells of another world
Of a tiny excitable pig-tailed girl
Whose hands made a tree house.
She lived like a wild animal in a wood
And made a river den and hid
And played with the boys and was never scared.
I sit and gaze and wonder
Her shake won't last forever
She can use my Mum's skin cream
And we'll cook her up a big meal.
So now I feel much better
I'm not going to ask her
I know she'll live forever,
She must, my Grandma, I love her.

Go to da clinic [*e*-motion]

I gotta trouble – da police
The law
I say stick it.
The teachers the same
I say they're all
In it.
But my mother and father they say you better change it
That face of you monster you'd better re-arrange it.

Chorus:
You go to da clinic
Put e-motion back in it
You go to da clinic
It's indifference that's in it
You go to da clinic
Put a smile back in it
You go to da clinic
Your face we rebuild it.

I got trouble with me nature
I was
Born with it.
And everything is negative no respect in it
Look at you like I want you to die – in'it
Everyone that's walking by – in'it
I don't even want to try – in'it
So my parents they say man get off to da clinic!

Chorus

I drive with me friends – we're speeding through it
I smoke with me friends – everyone do it
I run with me friends from the scene of the crime
Some gun may be killed and maybe next time?
I see me TV I see all the papers
No-one smiling no good news for us
Just the fighting and the-soapy-snore-us
Send us to sleep and deathly bore us!

Chorus

Hey! Stepped in da clinic got a fairy tale
Some people they was laughing
Someone gave me a smile
There wasn't any hate
There wasn't any vi-ol-ence
In the streets they're going to teach me to dance
Da clinic it's going to give peace a chance
Everyone going to take a new stance
Estonia, Latvia, Spain and France
The President dressed in his President's pants
Hey man we got a global romance!

Chorus

Night and day

The red sun he blushed
At the end of the day
And the stars they did wink
At him on his way.
The moon stretched her arms
Did yawn then arise
As a sea of black ink
Spilled on paper skies.

And a million bath tubs
Were filled 'cross the land
Millions of children
Were warm-washed by hand.
A trillion teeth
Were scrubbed white and clean
And their bright young owners
Were offered sweet dreams.

Then all were snuggled
Calm and still
And each one's head
Did slowly fill
With deepest dreams
All surprise
Of secret worlds
Behind those eyes.
Silence crept
And filled the walls

Moon and stars
Made shadows fall.
Parents slept
On king-size beds
Grown-ups with
Empty heads.

The golden sun was stirring
The start of a new day
Sleepy stars did close their eyes
And could not stay awake.
The silver moon was falling
Down below horizon
Now began her breakfast
Of warm moon dust and diamond.

So millions of children
Awoke across the land
And wondered at the miracle
Of their Creator's hand.

Thorax&Abdomen - The Bug Superstore

On our first floor
The finest footwear!
Hundreds of pairs for centipedes
Thousands of pairs for millipedes.
For spiders non-stick socks
Whilst surfing the web.
Genuine military boots
For the demanding soldier ant.
And an up-to-date range
Of all those fashion skates
Available in a range of water colours
For all pond-living creatures.
Calling all water boatmen
Why not get a move on?
Astride our skimmer skis
Live in the fast lane
Leave the oars behind
Move with the times.

On our second floor
Food for fanatics!
Leftovers of every kind
For all you hungry flies
We guarantee going off
You'll love eating with us.
Old meat for carnivores
New leaves for vegetarians.
Buzzing bees fill your basket

With a pollen pick-me-up.
Butterflies will flutter
Over a glass of our nectar.
For the dotty ladybird
With the busy lifestyle
A brimming bowl full
Of fresh formed aphids.
To aid your digestion
The soothing sound
Of our live band
The Chirping Cricket Sensation.

On our third floor
Yes, there's more!
Jewellery and fashion
So sparkle on reflection.
Cabbage Whites – is life a little dull?
Let our professional team
Turn you into a Painted Lady
With a little plastic surgery.
Go on give your mate
A real summer treat.
Spiders – too much leg hair?
Shave or braid yours here.
A full range of fashion
Cocoons for the conscious caterpillar.
Don't be eaten, get even!
Send those predators packing
A range of make-up
From the subtle to the shocking.

On our fourth floor
Worth waiting for!
Bugs'r'us tough toys
Buy or simply borrow,
Mommy – leave the larvae here
In our special crèche burrow.
By far the best in bug care
Your nymphs will be safe here.

It's a short life
Make the most of it.
You can throw it away
Wasting valuable retail time...

...Go on, make up your mind
Thorax & Abdomen
For all your insect needs,
From snails and spiders to flies and bees.

A swimming lesson

In our neighbourhood all the nice
Mums and Dads take their darlings swimming.
All the others encourage the arts
Of computer game playing
And television adoration
And, of course, drowning since
Their children have never been bathing.
In our neighbourhood all the little darlings
Run rings around their dizzy parents
And do some sword fencing
Jazz and tap and ballroom dancing,
Whilst their parents sit there gossiping
About the other parents, saying
What a parenting lesson
They could do with learning
And the difference between
Sinking and swimming.

Poo at the pool

A sudden change I did discern
Appeared upon young Lily's face
A sudden switch from serene smile
A thoughtful look, a true grimace.
Alarm bells ring inside my head
I stand up to attention
A grin on our young Lily's face
Tells tales too rude to mention.
No time to waste, I whisk her out
She sits upon the pool side.
Think quick, think quick, I tell myself
Nowhere to run, nowhere to hide.
To the shower! I command
We move with some aplomb
Together we can save the world
From Lily's hidden bomb.

Now guys, let me explain to you,
She is the youngest daughter,
Some things you can do in pools
And some things you ought no to.
"Daddy, she has done a poo!"
I beg them, "Not so loud",
Lily standing smiling there,
Of the poo she is so proud.
Repeating deep inside my head,
"Ladies – cool, gents – stay calm,
Nobody wants to hurt anybody

Nobody wants to come to harm."

I'm searching, then I catch it
I have it in my hand
The brown grenade I rush to save
And flush it down the pan.
"You have to clear the area,"
I hear the lifeguards say,
There's more where that came from
That deadly brown grenade.

Back at the explosive scene
I'm cleaning up again
Pushing all the shrapnel pieces
Down the shower drain.
And so the bomb disposal squad
Has saved the day once more.
We salute you swimming public
We keep clean your pool
And Lily, you're diffused now
It's time to bathe again
We can swim in safety
Down at the shallow end.

Teacher's cauldron

Eye of toad and leg of frog
Spines of prickly hedgehog.
Insides of slug, his sticky slime
The black bits of maggots all crawling in line.
Heads of spiders crunchy and black
Wriggling worm front and back.
Greenfly, blackfly, cockroach shell
Rotting eggs and their foul smell.
A pinch of brain, a little ear
A toenail there, a toenail here.
Bluebottle tongue, jellyfish jelly
Fatty bits of fatty belly.
Mealy grub and crocodile
Dogfish, catfish, squirming eel.
Piggy's trotter, kidney, liver
Slippery fish skins shining silver.
Nose of dog and cheek of cat
Wing of crow and tail of bat.
One hundred crawling caterpillars
A thousand snails with gooey innards
All steamed in breath from stagnant pond
Mixed up with my magic wand.
Black and thick, oh deadly drink
Tell me children what you think.
So my pretties take a look
Attention please, put down your books
Your pencils and your paper too
Scissors, paint and sticky glue.

Now look straight into teacher's eye
Repeat these words beginning with "I
Will always pay attention
Do as my teacher asks
I'll go about things quietly
Never chatter in class.
I'll never fidget, never fuss
Courteous, so polite
Never pull of scratch or punch
And never pick a fight.
Always patient loving child
Never mean and snappy
The most important think each day
To make my teacher happy."
Or else my pretties
I'll take a cup
And make you drink
The whole lot up!
Delicious drink from teacher's cauldron
Special brew for naughty children.

Killer Skimmer

A boy in danger

A boy who holds the future

In an uncertain hand

He scours the land

Combing the sands

He has the plan

A boy, a decision

A moment, a mission

A boy like no other

Strange, a loner

He hides undercover

Until, one day, the waiting – is over

Juan-Carlos-Jesus-Iglesius-Sanchez is
Killer Skimmer

Hide if you will but there's only one winner

The Killer Skimmer

Co-starring
Anna-Maria-Rosita-Bonita-Real-Madrida
Skimmer's only friend

A beautiful girl

With a dark secret

And dyed blonde hair

She has the looks

He has no brains

A story of love, hate

And finally revenge...

Ah! Look out Mommy it's Killer Skimmer
Don't be so silly junior
Why he's only a kid
With a beautiful girl
Look out Mommy it's him
Don't be so silly calm down
Junior's right Ma'am
I am Killer Skimmer
But right now I have a stone in my hand
Right now I'm a dangerous man

Co-co-starring many other people
With unpronounceable Spanish names

Buena Vista Pictures present
Killer Skimmer
Life and death
There's only one winner.

Plea from a tube of toothpaste

Twist my neck
And hear me groan
You should leave
This tube alone.
Strangle me
Again again
And hear me
Crying out in pain.
Torture me
'Twixt finger, thumb
Squeeze me senseless
Feel me numb.
Leave me wrecked
By side of sink
Take a minute
Please do think.
I do not mind
My bottom pinched
I draw the line
At being lynched.

Don't run me over

Chorus:
Don't run me over
I'm a famous writer
So many wondrous words
I've left to say.
Don't run me over
I'd be kind of dead, yeah
The people need to
Hear my voice today!

Every now and then
It seems a genius is born
All the angels up in Heaven
They were singin' on that morn
They cried "well hallelujah
A saviour is he"
I was born to save the world
You know I mean that literally!

Chorus

Some children they just love to play
Well that is fair enough
But me I couldn't wait
To get working on all that stuff
At six months I was talking
At age one I could write
At eight I'm reading Tolstoy
Got Shakespeare in my sights.

Chorus

Now other kids went dancin'
And had a lot of fun
But me I like to stay at home
A-sharpening my pen.
I learnt to speak in Latin
I thought in ancient Greek
I took my dictionary to bed
To help me off to sleep.

Chorus

Now I didn't have much money
I was penniless and poor
Till I had a story published
They said hey we want some more!
Hey guys this guy is gold dust
I was the biggest hit
Now I'm selling millions
And I'm living like a king.

Chorus

And now I'm writing poetry
And novels by the score
Film scripts, plays and TV sets
And sure there's much much more.
When God was handing gifts out
He gave the pen to me
And when I get to Heaven
I'll write his biography.

Chorus

Banks

I sauntered down the main street
In search of spending money
'Tis here I came upon a bank
Financial milk and honey.

I entered by the sawdust door
Was knocked down by the smell
I thought, "There's something strange in here,
But what I cannot tell."

I waited by the cash desk
I was about to meet
A fellow with a huge snout
Long ears and trotter feet.

"My fellow I would like some notes,"
I asked of this fat lump
"I do believe you've got it wrong,"
He answered with a grunt.

"This here is a piggy bank
No notes but ham alone
And when you want to take some out
We carve it off the bone."

I left there in a hurry
And next what did I see
A smartly suited gentleman
Who looked like you and me.

But great loads of glass he carried
He swore it was no prank
He'd tried to take some cash out
Down at the bottle bank.

Soap gets in your eyes

All of you children
Scared of shampoo
Don't listen to adults
Here's what you must do,

Don't tip your head back
No rinsing the sides
It's sure to creep forward
And swim in your eyes.
Don't trust the bubbles
Bursting with lies
Pop up your nosie
And sting in your eyes.
Don't wear the flannel
It is no surprise
A flannel can't stop it
The soap in your eyes.
It won't last a second
This white foaming tide
But oh! How it hurts!
Soap *stays* in your eyes.
All of you children
We know it's the truth
Shampoo can kill you
Here's what you must do:
Don't take a shower
Nor in a bath bathe
When water laps round you

It's time to escape,
Admit you're a coward
Go run and hide
Some place where the shampoo
Can't get in your eyes.

St. Jenkins and the dragon

End of term in sleepy staff-room
Headmaster's deciding on who will teach whom.
"Who would like 5C next year?"
Teachers shrink then disappear.
"Jenkins you look just the chap,
Young and fit and bold as brass."
"Oh no sir, I think you're clearly mistaken,"
Said Jenkins secretly trembling and shaking.
"Oh no Jenkins, I don't think I am,
Look at you Jenkins, you're just the man."

"But sir I'm barely five feet tall
Forty kilos of skin and bone."
"Aha! But it's the strength of mind
Jenkins you are one of a kind
So that's it decided, Jenkins – 5C,"
And Jenkins could not disagree.

Summer passed, September came
Headmaster welcomed school again.
"5C you've a real treat,"
(Mr. Jenkins on his feet)
And 5C they did awful grin
And Mr. Jenkins sank within.

"Now Jenkins just before you start –
A word about your lovely class.
They're difficult, a lively bunch

They like to wrestle, kick and punch
But Jenkins I know you can tame
The class that likes to kill and maim.
Cheer up Jenkins, smiling face!
Take this with you just in case,
Put it on, salute me do,
Jenkins here's your new classroom."

Jenkins just as he had planned
Met 5C sword in right hand,
Suit of armour to protect
Shield held fast in his left
Visor shut at register
He mumbles and they shout out "Sir!"

All is still and calm and steady
Catapults loaded at the ready,
Cannon filled and arrows strung
And maths has only just begun.
Jenkins turns to face 5C
To stand up to the enemy.

'Tis then the arrows fill the air
The hapless Jenkins standing there
A target for the boiling tar
Missiles rain from near and far.
He wants to teach a little maths –
"Now let's be reasonable class."
He lifts his shield, he clasps his sword
He carries on without a word.

But finally the shotgun sounded
The suit of armour – Jenkins – grounded
And dragged away from battle scene
To staff-room and a cup of tea.

"Well done Jenkins, quite a battle
After break, you'll see, they'll settle
And Jenkins I will have inscribed
These words upon our notice board..."

'JENKINS – NO MORE BRAVER KNIGHT THAN HE
WHO FOUGHT THE MONSTER – CLASS 5C.'

Lynn limericks

There was a young man from West Lynn
Who was drinking extremely strong gin
When I drink I can't think
He said with a wink
So pour me another agin.

There was a young man from West Lynn
Who made such a terrible din
I'm loud and I'm proud
He exclaimed to the crowd
And then put his hearing aid in.

There was a young girl from West Lynn
Who had an enormous long chin
I'm not having this
She said to the nurse
Who said, "Where's it end and begin."

The Chocolate Doctor

The chocolate doctor looked at me
Stroked his chin so thoughtfully.
"Kindly do remove your vest
I must examine the patient's chest."
"Oh Chocolate Doctor - there's something wrong!"
"Do lie back and let me get on!
Now when will you trust in me?"
He said, his face so chocolate sweet.
"Oh Doctor, yes indeed I do
You and your chocolate answers too.
See your chocolate skin it shines
As cocoa pulses through your veins
Oh Doctor how I do so wish
Like you I might look such a dish."

"Now let me help you, let me listen."
(His chocolate eyes did smile and glisten)
His stethoscope cold on my skin
He shook his head and stroked his chin.
His chocolate egg head he did shake
And on the couch in boots I quake.
"Is it Doctor? Tell me the worst!
Must I start planning my funeral at once?"
Silence – at length the Doctor replied,
"Time I'm afraid is not on our side.
Your heart is weak, your skin is pale,
Your guts are bad, your liver will fail.
You blood it's white, your oxygen low,

Your bones are brittle, your teeth yellow.
Your chocolate count is the lowest yet
You clearly have been neglecting yourself!"

"Here, now listen to my prescription
'Tis chocolate of every description.
Cold chocolate in the morning,
Hot chocolate late at night.
A chocolate bar on every hour
Top up as required.
Chocolate for your dinner
Chocolate for your tea.
Chocolate liquid, chocolate solid
Chocolate as you please."

"A chocolate drip we'll set up
We'll start this very day
Emergency infusion
We'll give you right away."
"Doctor will I make it?
Will I pull on through?
Tell me! I don't want to die!
I want to look like you!
"I don't want to promise
It's so difficult to say
But let the chocolate do its thing
Let's hope its not too late."
I closed my tired eyes
Submitted to the spell
I trust the Chocolate Doctor

I know all will be well.
I felt the chocolate in me
A power to my spirit
Above the planet I did soar
The chocolate took me with it.

Six months on I'm still alive
And you'll wish you had skin like mine
Chocolate brown from head to toe
Healthy glisten, shiny glow.
My bones, my blood, my liver and teeth
The perfect picture of chocolate health.

So may I recommend to you
The next time you are feeling blue
Pasty white and all washed out
Shadows creep and fill with doubt
Stress and labour, all is strife
Start again – this chocolate life!

Lipstick

Luscious and full
But too much lippy
Just a bit, see
Moist and slippy
Lose my grippy
What a pity
I know they're pretty.
But far too tricky
Wet and drippy.
Too much spitty
Bit more gritty
Nice and nippy
In a jiffy
Wipe the lippy
Honey – kiss me!

The wasp

Hot afternoon, sunny June
When wasp flies straight
Into our classroom.
Teacher says be sensible
Do not move
Quiet as a mouse
Still as stone
He's only a wasp
Let's all be calm.
But Samantha who is the silliest girl
In our class (and probably the whole world)
Giggling, fidgeting, making a fuss
Disturbed herself starts the rest of us.
"Samantha, sit down on your bottom at once!"
But Samantha is running from our friend the wasp.
Samantha starts Sadie who fluffs up her hair
And shrieks at the wasp she thinks is in there.
Says that her pigtails will fall out of place
And she will no longer be a princess
"Sadie stop fussing, my fragile child
I'm sure that your delicate frame won't be spoiled."

Then looney Billy gets in on the act
Likes to kill everything, totally mad
Starts swishing and swiping the air around him
His hard eyes a-gleaming, his monstrous grin.
Nervous Nick who sits next to Billy
Can't help himself and starts acting silly

He's read too many books on war
Says wasp is a bomber who'll give him what for.
"Watch out," he screams his guns are loaded
Wasp he dive-bombed and Nicky exploded.
"It's not funny you all heard the drone,
He's about to drop the big one don't leave me all alone."
Now hear the tale-tellers to add to the woe
Millions of stories of waspee gung ho!
Of kids who were stung in the mouth and the eyes
Bites that poisoned, maimed and paralysed
Big bites that swell to the football size
Stung kids in hospital, stung kids who died.
Now nervous Nick is jumpier than ever
Looney Billy has wasp-killing fever
Samantha she hides in the corner of the room
And Sadie she shrieks "I'm not coming to school!
It's a frightening place and no-one cares
Look at the tears and the state of my hair."
"It's alright for you, see I'm going to die,"
And Nick points to the wasp which is dive-bombing by.

Then it's the turn of the toady class helpers
The good-goodies who'll save the class from the chaos.
Don't worry Nick, Billy, Samantha and Sadie
We're the class helpers and we've come to save ye.
We'll finish the wasp, here come the swatters
They're cutting the air with their rolled up jotters
And now the class rises and joins in as one
The beginning of the end of our class has begun.
Everyone running and shouting and waving

Bumping and smashing and crying and wailing
And moaning and groaning with tears in their eyes
And shoving and pushing to win the wasp prize.

Then all of a sudden Miss screams, "That's enough!"
But it's not and the class carry on with their stuff
Deaf to Miss' screams and the voices of reason
And mad for a wasp in the wasp-hunting season.
So Miss tries again and stands on the chair
And jumps up and down to tell us she's there.
She's red-faced, she's crying, hysterical too
She's barking out orders, here's what you should do,
"Go back to your places, sit down, do not move!
Everyone silent – do not breathe a word.
Do not breathe a word or I'll squash you as well!"
Serious we see, by her red face we tell.
"OK class, there's just one last chance,"
Up on the sill Miss is starting to dance.
She moves toward window open wide too
Then bends down a little, she's going on through!
She's flapping her arms and pretending to fly
We're stunned into silence, will Miss have a try?
And leap to the shiny black tarmac below
Break every one of her beautiful bones?
Then Nervous Nick shouts, "No, Miss don't do it!"
And Mad Billy – well he's really lost it!
Doing the wasp dance and buzzing about
But Sadie can't see what the fuss is about.
Just look at me, I'm a terrible mess
Samantha has hidden her head in her desk.

"I will I'll do it!" shouts Miss from her perch
"You've driven me to it you miserable bunch."
And one of her legs is out of the window
The other is following surely but slowly.
Time ticks by in a dreadful slow motion
Even Mad Billy has ceased his commotion.
And none – not one – can really believe this
How one tiny insect could end it for Miss
And now we're all praying but Miss does not bluff
Miss on the ledge she's about to jump off.

Seconds left to save her life
When up jumps a toady just in good time
And shows Miss the head of the foulsome wasp
The rest of the body all broken and crushed.
Miss looks at the present, then blank-eyed stares
And a hush descends and no-one dares
Hope that Miss might change her mind
And slowly and surely she starts to climb.
On this hot afternoon, sunny June
Miss crawls back
Into our classroom.
Class says be sensible
Do not move
Quiet as a mouse
Still as a stone.
She's only a teacher
Let's all be calm.

La pintora

Lily, aged a little
Less that two
Has something of interest
To show you.
It's a perfect painted
Clean white wall
No other colour
None at all.

Lily aged one and
Quite a bit
Discovers the wall and
Puzzles with it.
At the plain and
Dull and monochrome
This wall needs some colour
A life all of its own.

Lily aged one and
Not quite two
Says I can do
The job for you.
For I young Lily
Have the tools
A creative mind
And crayons too.

Lily aged one and

Quite a lot
Picks up her pencils
And gives it a shot.
Yellow, red, a little
Green
Black and blue and
In between.

Lily this artiste of
Tender age
Colours the canvas like
Wax on a page.
And whilst we are sleeping
Moves on to another
To cover the white
With some bright Lily colour.

We wake to a new dawn
We see and discover
The walls of our home
Are not like any other.
And Lily aged a little
Less than two
Will decorate
Your home for *you.*

London

I mustn't be ready for London
I'm still smiling at everyone
I can't be ready for London
I'm still feeling human
Put the fun back into London
Do up what's been undone
Put the fun back into London
Escape the web you've spun.
I'm not ready for London
I'm too human
I'm not ready for London
I'm smiling at everyone.
You're not ready for me London.
Smile, armed with facial stun gun
Under London's bloody setting sun
Gonna paint this town human.

Summer's song

Summer's song sang surreal skies
Certain blue swallows swoop and dive.
Set scene of yellow sun sheen
Silver sea surface glistening.
Standing still this Summer seems
Stored inside, my sweet soul sings.
Summer's song surprises, smiles
Spirit says Summer secret sidles
So Summer said and simmering
Sank sunlight's shadows shimmering.

A lickle bit of Lily

Lily this sullen Sunday morning
This day without the sun is drowning
Draw the curtains – by and by
The sun has fled the sky to hide.

Come on sun come out to play
Don't be shy and hide away
Come on sun we have a treat
Lots of cloud for you to eat.

Lots of dew for you to drink
Come on sun give us a wink
And how about a little smile
To light our hearts a little while.

Me and Lily from her bedroom
Stare forth into murky gloom
At leaden dirty grey smudge Heaven
And muddy gardens puddle sodden.

Tarmac dull and dingy wet
Neighbours damp-proofed sleep in bed
And drizzle slowly by and by
Nails up this coffin sky.

I know – it's hide and seek you're playing
Close our eyes and hear us saying
Hundred, coming ready or not!
We're coming sun, we're getting hot!

And hot and hotter still
You're hiding underneath our sill!
For that is where the sunshine shines
No parking – double *yellow* lines!

Little girl

The little girl laughed
The little girl smiled
And the shoppers stopped dead
In their tracks for a while.

The little girl vision
Made such a surprise
A glimpse of our beauty
Through childhood's eyes.

Fairy tale reflection
In miniature, her face
Takes us softly by her hand
On to a sacred place.

Senses are sharpened
Streaming colours bright
Playground is the daytime
Cosy is the night.

We chased our kites
In far off fields
We slept sound on
Soft cotton sheets.

We played all day
Beneath a sun
Our pulse beat joy
Our blood ran fun.

The little girl stopped
To look in our hearts
And mend all the broken
The pain and the hurt.

Endless questions
Ceaseless strife
Lessons learnt
From adult life.

We picked up our packages
One by one
The little girl left
And time moved on.

Why children don't like poetry

There were loads of children's books
In the shop
Millions of children's books sleeping on shelves
In the shop
Novel books, board books, novelty books age five to
twelve
In that shop.
Have you got any poetry in your shop?
She thinks and stops
On the very bottom nearest the dirty carpet
She says with a tut.
I see titles on the subjects of toilets, bums and farts
And I nod.
Excuse me but aren't there any proper poetry books?
And the lady stops.
No, unless you can think of some.
Well actually, I write them
Can I put my proper poetry books on your poetry shelf?
My dear I'm afraid it's not long enough.
Can't you ask the manager if we might use another?
I can see I've clearly annoyed her.
You don't understand, you haven't a clue
You don't understand the money, do you?
Publishers have decided children don't read poems any
more.
And a person who writes poems which children won't read
Quietly slipped out through the door.

Station-master's prayer

Ladies and gentlemen
Welcome to my station!
De train arriving at platform 1
Is de train for all stations
To London Paddington-
Leaving from dis platform.
Ladies and gentlemen-
Dis is de train
(I'll say it again)
Dis train is
Via Stoke-on-Trent
To Birmingham
For London.
Dis is de train
Via Birmingham
To London
Paddington.
Ladies and gentlemen-
Dis is de train
(I'll say it again)
Dis is de London train
De train for London Paddington
Calling at all stations
Via Stoke-on-Trent
And Birmingham
Ladies and gentlemen-
Amen.

Guess the age

I asked my Grandpa so I did
Why the gaps, the missing teeth?
Them said Grandpa are a sign of wisdom
I'm old and wise now, I don't need them.

I asked my Grandpa so I did
Why wear glasses can't you see?
Them said Grandpa are to aid my vision
Tired old eyes lack boyhood precision.

I asked my Grandpa so I did
About the wrinkles on his skin.
Those said Grandpa are a tell-tale sign
Your Grandpa here is an ancient man.

Grandpa how old exactly are you?
You remember the dinosaurs don't you?
And days before electricity
Cave painting and no TV.

Woolly mammoth, horse and cart
Buses, trams and steam-driven cars.
I do said Grandpa long time ago
When I was about as old as you.

Yes but Grandpa when was it please?
More or less than a thousand years?
Eh? said Grandpa can't be sure
Maybe hundred maybe more.

But listen lad I can't remember
You'd better ask another fella
Dim and distant, passed by me
My mind's not what it was you see.

Sad, Grandpa turns and looks aside.
But Grandpa you're too young to die!
(I can't catch my Grandpa's eye)
Oh aye, he nods, oh aye he smiles.

I tell you what though, when I'm dead
You can take a look inside me legs
And count the rings – just like a tree
The secret years I've hidden in me.

It's not fair

Chorus:
It's not fair, it's not fair
I've been moaning all my life
Are you out there?
We don't care, we don't care
So there, yeah, yeah,
Yeah, yeah, yeah yeah!

Nobody loved me
Nobody even cared
No wonder I'm a failure
No wonder I'm so scared.

I never got the chocolate
I never got the cake
I never got the sweety things
'Cos Mummy couldn't bake.

Chorus

I never had the presents
We never had the money
A life like sour vinegar
The others' sweet as honey.

I never had the good looks
I always had the spots
I never had a girlfriend
The others took the lot.

Chorus

I never had the brains
I never liked the school
I never thought of anything
'Cos thinking wasn't cool.

And now I've got a long life
I'm never ever ill
Will this go on forever?
Well that's the bitter pill.

Chorus

And when I get to Heaven
I'll have a word with God
I'll tell him life – it wasn't fair
He'll smile at me and nod.
And all the angels will sing along...
It's not fair, it's not fair
I've been moaning all my life
Are you out there?
We don't care, we don't care
So there, yeah, yeah,
Yeah, yeah, yeah yeah!

Heavens above (and look out below)

I was a little bored one day
So I said to myself
Why not have a flight up there
To look on Heaven's shelves?
I might just surprise myself
You never know what's there
Ask God for the key, he'll give it to me
And show me up the stairs
Oh, oh, oh...

Chorus:
Cumulo nimbus, cirrus and stratus, warm front, cold front,
freeze!
Bring on the clouds, those woolly mounds and shape them just
for me
The stars by night, the sun by day
The heavens all around
Dancing and a-singing
We float above the ground
Oh, oh, oh, oh,
Oh, oh, oh, oh...

So I purchased an aeroplane
And flew it through the skies
I'd flown just an hour or two
When something met my eye
Well I did surprise myself
And guess whom did I find
God gave me the wink, said what do you think
Come on and take a ride

Oh, oh, oh...

Chorus

I was a trifle nervous
I'd not done this before
But God said not to worry
I'd soon pick up the score
Yes you will surprise yourself
The music's made for you
I picked up the tune and very very soon
I'm dancing oop-pe-dooh!
Oh, oh, oh...

Chorus

Now let me tell you people
I'd never dreamed of this
But God said that I'm so good
I am too good to miss
Yes you have surprised yourself
You clearly have a skill
By the silver moonlight I practice each night
Oh what a heavenly thrill!
Oh, oh, oh...

Chorus

I met up with the angels
I thought they played the harp
But no they just like dancing
Oh boy and what a lark!

Yes they have surprised themselves
Worked hard on their routine
One look at me, they said well gee
Come on and join our team!
Oh, oh, oh...

Chorus

Now I'm dancing all day long
And all the night time too
I hop from cloud to sun and back
And skip across the moon
Yes we have surprised ourselves
The angels' team and me
One flip of our wings, God pulls the strings
Good-bye to gravity
Oh, oh, oh...

Chorus

Now folks if you're feeling bored
Here's what you should do
Come up to Heaven
And join our party too
Yes we'll all surprise ourselves
At last we will be free
We'll dance and sing and do our thing
The angels you and me
Oh, oh, oh...

Chorus